2018 Wiley

CPAexcel®
EXAM REVIEW
FOCUS NOTES

Wiley

2018 CPAexcel® EXAM REVIEW

FOCUS NOTES

REGULATION

WILEY

CONTENTS

v

Contents

Contents

Contents

Contents

Contents   **X**

PREFACE

This publication is a comprehensive yet simplified study program. It provides a review of all the basic skills and concepts tested on the CPA exam and teaches important strategies to take the exam faster and more accurately. This tool allows you to take control of the CPA exam.

This simplified and focused approach to studying for the CPA exam can be used:

- As a handy and convenient reference manual
- To solve exam questions
- To reinforce material being studied

Included is all of the information necessary to obtain a passing score on the CPA exam in a concise and easy-to-use format. Due to the wide variety of information covered on the exam, a number of techniques are included:

- Acronyms and mnemonics to help you learn and remember a variety of rules and checklists
- Formulas and equations that simplify complex calculations required on the exam
- Simplified outlines of key concepts without the details that encumber or distract from learning the essential elements

- Techniques that can be applied to problem solving or essay writing, such as preparing a multiple-step income statement, determining who will prevail in a legal conflict, or developing an audit program
- Pro forma statements, reports, and schedules that make it easy to prepare these items by simply filling in the blanks
- Proven techniques to help you become a smarter, sharper, and more accurate test taker

This publication may also be useful to university students enrolled in Intermediate, Advanced, and Cost Accounting classes; Auditing, Business Law, and Federal Income Tax classes; or Economics and Finance classes.

PROFESSIONAL AND LEGAL RESPONSIBILITIES

Treasury Department Circular 230

Establishes requirements for practicing before the Internal Revenue Service (IRS)

- Requires registration with the IRS
- Accountant must promptly provide records and documents to the IRS unless the accountant believes the information is privileged
- If accountant becomes aware of error in filed tax return must notify client of error and consequences of not filing an amended return
- Accountant must exercise due diligence in preparing tax return
- Accountant must not charge an unconscionable fee
- Accountant must not negotiate or endorse a client's government refund check
- Accountant must possess adequate competence to perform an assignment
- Accountants with responsibility for overseeing a tax practice must take adequate steps to ensure compliance by all personnel

Treasury Department Circular 230 (continued)

- Accountant may rely on information obtained from client without verification but must make additional inquiries if information appears incorrect, incomplete or inconsistent with the facts
- Accountants have additional responsibilities when providing written advice

Liability as a Tax Preparer

Penalties

Actions by an accountant preparing a client's tax return can result in penalties

- Not providing client with copy of return
- Failing to sign return as a preparer
- Endorsing and cashing client's refund check

Liability to Client

Other actions may create a liability to a tax client

- Failing to file a return timely
- Not advising client of tax elections
- Neglecting evaluation of joint versus separate returns

Regulation of Accountants

- State boards of accountancy issue licenses to practice in a state
  - Investigate violations of professional standards and ethics
  - May revoke license to practice
- AICPA and state societies of CPAs
  - Investigate violations of professional ethics through Joint Ethics Enforcement Program (JEEP)
  - May admonish, sanction, suspend, or expel a member
- The AICPA Uniform Accountancy Act (UAA)
  - Provides guidance to states in establishing accountancy laws
  - Contains rules for education, reciprocity, continuing education, etc.

Regulation of Accountants (continued)

- The Securities Exchange Commission
  - Investigates CPAs and CPA firms that violate SEC rules
  - May disbar an accountant or firm from auditing public (issuer) companies
- The Public Company Accounting Oversight Board (PCAOB)
  - Registers and performs inspections of firms that audit public (issuer) companies
  - Firms that audit more than 100 issuers are inspected every year
  - Firms that audit 100 or less issuers are inspected every three years
  - For substandard performance the PCAOB may:
    - Prescribe remedial actions such as improvements in quality control
    - Suspend an individual or firm from auditing issuers

Accountants' Liability

Liability under Common Law

An accountant may be liable under common law due to negligence or fraud.

Negligence

A loss due to negligence occurs when an accountant violates the duty to perform professional services in a competent manner. **NEG**ligence may consist of

- **N**ondisclosure of information to a client
- **E**rrors previously discovered not being corrected
- **G**AAP not being followed

Best defense to common law negligence is that appropriate professional standards were followed.

Negligence (continued)

Simple negligence

- Careless mistakes
- Defense of lack of privity may be available

  - But client and intended third-party beneficiaries have privity
  - Foreseen third parties have privity in majority of states under tort law
  - Foreseen third parties lack privity in states conforming to Ultramares case

Gross negligence

- Reckless disregard for the truth
- Lack of privity not valid as defense

Fraud

Fraud refers to conduct that involves all of the following:

- Material **f**alse representation of fact
- Justifiable **r**eliance on the information
- **A**wareness of the false information by the accountant
- The falsity was made with the **u**ltimate intent to deceive
- The party must have suffered **d**amages

Scienter refers to the accountant's knowledge of a false representation or material omission of fact with the intent to deceive.

Potential defenses against fraud include:

- Lack of intent to deceive
- Immateriality

Lack of privity is not a valid defense.

Tax Preparer Penalties

Minor violations

- Failure to provide the taxpayer's identifying number on the return
- Endorse or negotiate a refund check
- Fail to sign return as preparer
- Fail to provide client with copy of filed return
- Fail to keep copies of client returns for at least three years
- Fail to keep list for at least three years of employees preparing returns
- Failing to exercise due diligence in determining if a taxpayer is eligible for the earned income credit
- Basing fees on a percentage of the refund amount or computing fees using any figure from tax returns.

Major violations

- Understatement of tax liability due to an undisclosed position for which there is not substantial authority (at least 40% probability of success): penalty is greater of $1,000 or 50% of income to be derived from return or claim
- Willful attempt to understate tax liability, or intentional or reckless disregard of rules and regulations; penalty is greater of $5,000 or 75% of income to be derived from return or claim

Tax Preparer Penalties (continued)

No violation

- Adequate disclosure and a showing that there was a reasonable basis (at least 20% probability of success) for the position
- Reasonable cause for the understatement and the preparer acted in good faith
- Use estimates when client did not maintain adequate records
- Rely on information supplied by client not appearing incorrect or inconsistent

Liability under Federal Securities Regulations

Auditors are liable under both the Securities Act of 1933 (33 Act) and the Securities Exchange Act of 1934 (34 Act).

Liability under 33 Act

Accountants are liable under Section 11 of the 33 Act

- Liable if financial statements contain untrue statement or material omission
- Liable to anyone acquiring security without knowledge of error

To be successful, the plaintiff need not prove

- Privity
- Scienter
- Reliance

Defenses the accountant may use include

- Plaintiff's knowledge of the error
- Due diligence in performance of services

AGENCY

Authority of Agents and Principals

Agent works on behalf of the principal

Agent owes fiduciary duty to the principal to act in the principal's best interests; fiduciary duties include duty of

- Loyalty
- Obedience
- Due care

Terminating Agent's Authority

Authority of agent terminates in certain cases

- Agreement—Principal and agent agree to end of authority
- Unilateral—Principal dismisses agent or agent resigns
  - Actual authority terminated even if in breach of contract
- Operation of law—Death, insanity, incapacity, or illegality of subject matter of agency

Apparent authority can still exist, unless authority was terminated by operation of law, then all authority is terminated

Principal can avoid responsibility of agent's subsequent (after termination) acts by giving

- Personal notice to third parties who dealt with agent
- Public (also known as constructive) notice for all others
- Notice not required when termination is by operation of law

Liability

Generally, principals can be held liable for the actions of their agents, but principals are not responsible for the actions of independent contractors.

Contract Liability

If the third party is suing the principal/agent for breach of contract, then consider what authority the agent had to enter into the contract and the disclosure status of the principal.

	Actual Authority	Apparent Authority	No Authority
Disclosed principal	Principal (P) only	P only	Agent (A) only
Partially disclosed	P and/or A	P and/or A	A only
Undisclosed	P or A, not both	Cannot exist	A only

Tort Liability

- If agent commits a tort while in the scope of the principal's employment, then the third party holds the principal liable, or the agent liable, or both the principal and agent liable; this is joint and several liability.
- If agent commits a tort outside the scope of employment, then only the agent is liable.

CONTRACTS

Formation of Contracts

Elements

In order to form a valid contract, there are three required elements

1. **O**ffer
2. **A**cceptance
3. **C**onsideration

> With all three elements, a contract is as sturdy as an **oac** (okay, so it should be oak) tree.

Offer

Expresses intent to enter into contract

To be effective, the offer must be definite as to terms and received by the offeree

To be **definite**, an offer generally includes

- Price
- Subject matter
- Time for performance
- Terms considered definite if reasonable person could determine them

An offer may be revoked at any time until accepted

- A promise to hold an offer open for a specified time is not binding unless supported by consideration
- A revocation is effective when received by the offeree

Acceptance

Acceptance is generally effective when dispatched (mailbox rule)

Not effective until received when

- Offer so specifies
- Accepted by unauthorized means
- Sent by means not equal to or better than that used to communicate offer

Acceptance must be the same terms as offer (mirror image rule)

- A modification represents a counteroffer
- Initial offer is rejected and offeree makes a new offer

Rejection

Rejection of an offer is effective when received by the offeror

- Terminates original offer
- If rejection is followed by acceptance, whichever is received first is effective

Consideration

Given in exchange for promise to form contract

Must be legally sufficient

- Bargained for: One promise induces the other promise
- Legal value: Party agrees to do something that s/he is otherwise not obligated to do, or refraining from an action that the party has a legal right to do
- Does not have to be of equal value

Consideration may take various forms

- May involve forfeiting a legal right
- May be performed by a third party
- May not consist of past performance or preexisting obligation

Writing and Records

Enforceability

Under the Statute of Frauds, executory must be in writing, or have written evidence, to be enforceable. These include

- A **g**uarantee of the debt of another
- A sale of **g**oods for $500 or more
- A contract that cannot be completed within **o**ne year
- A contract involving an interest in **l**and

LEGGY, **E**xecutory promises for **L**and, **G**oods, **G**uaranteeing another's debts, and that cannot be completed within one **Y**ear need a writing.

If the contract itself is not in writing, then a sufficient writing is a writing or combination of writings that

- Identifies the parties to the contract,
- Identifies the terms of the contract, and
- Contains the signature of the party to be charged (sued)

Parol Evidence Rule

Oral evidence generally cannot be used to contradict a written contract. The Rule excludes

- Negotiations and agreements prior to the written contract
- Oral agreements occurring at the same time as the written agreement

The Rule allows

- Oral agreements occurring after the written agreement
- Clarification of ambiguous terms in the written agreement
- Evidence that the contract was void or voidable

Validity and Enforceability

In certain circumstances, no valid contract exists. Even if a contract exists, it may not be enforceable.

- A condition precedent is a condition that must be met before a contract becomes enforceable
- A condition subsequent is a condition that, upon being met, releases a party from obligation

Validity

Certain factors may indicate that there is no valid contract

Fraud—A party entering into a contract due to a fraudulent misrepresentation will not be held to it. The contract is

- Void due to fraud in the execution (deceived into thinking it isn't a contract)
- Voidable due to fraud in the inducement

Ability—A party that does not have the capacity to enter into a contract will not be held to it

- The contract is generally voidable.
- The party may ratify or disaffirm the contract upon obtaining capacity.

Influence—A party entering a contract due to being improperly influenced (undue influence) may not be held to it. The contract is voidable.

Validity (continued)

Legality—A party entering into an illegal contract will generally not be held to it. The contract is void.

- Violation of a licensing statute designed to raise revenues does not make the contract illegal.
- Violation of a licensing statute designed to protect the public does make the contract illegal.

Error—A party entering into a contract by mistake will generally not be held to it. The contract is

- Voidable in the case of mutual mistake (both parties were in error)
- Unenforceable when the other party should have recognized the mistake or when there is a material clerical error

Duress or force—A party forced to sign a contract will not be held to it. The contract is

- Void if the duress is extreme, such as immediate threat of physical harm
- Voidable if the duress is simple, such as a threat of breaching a contract

*These are the reasons the contract **failed**.*

Discharge of Performance

A party may also be released from obligations by being discharged. Discharge can result from a variety of circumstances.

- Satisfactory performance
- A condition precedent was not met
- The contract was rescinded
- An accord and satisfaction—Different performance is accepted in place of the contracted for performance

Discharge may also occur as an operation of law.

- Performance becomes impossible
- Death or incapacity of the obligated party when personal services are required by that party under the contract
- Discharge in bankruptcy
- Illegality of the obligation

Breach of Contract

Nonperformance, resulting in a breach of contract, changes the relationship between the parties.

1) A material breach by one party releases the other.
2) Most breaches are nonmaterial; the remedy is normally compensatory damages.
3) One may inform the other that they will not perform resulting in an anticipatory breach of contract. The other party could
   - Cancel the contract
   - Sue for compensatory damages immediately

Damages

An injured party may seek damages.

Money damages may include

- Compensatory damages to recover losses
- Consequential damages cover indirect costs and anticipated losses, but are only available if they are foreseeable to the breaching party
- Punitive damages are not available for breach of contract
- Nominal damages ($1) are awarded when the nonbreaching party fails to prove damages.
- Liquidated damage clauses specify the amount an injured party will receive; such clauses are enforceable if the specified damages are reasonable.

Specific performance, requiring the other party to perform their obligations, may be appropriate when the subject of the contract is unique, such as real estate.

An action resulting from breach must be brought within the time period specified in the relevant **statute of limitations**.

Passage of Title and Risk Loss

Title

Contract may specify when title passes to buyer.

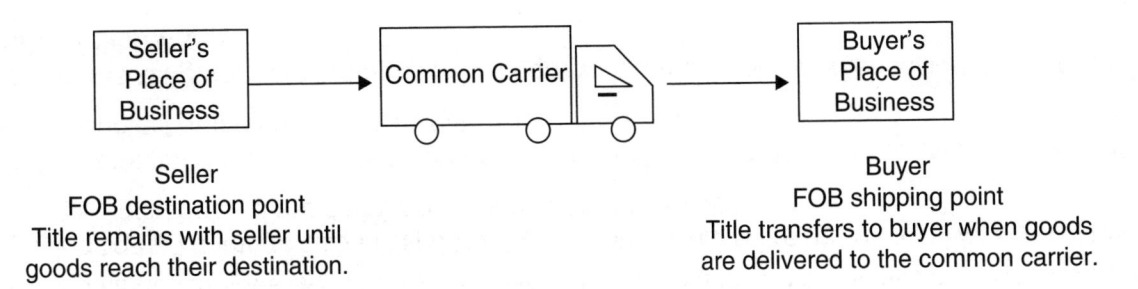

Seller
FOB destination point
Title remains with seller until
goods reach their destination.

Buyer
FOB shipping point
Title transfers to buyer when goods
are delivered to the common carrier.

When goods are not delivered

- Title passes when document of title is delivered
- In absence of document of title, title passes when goods have been identified to the contract

Title (continued)

Title transfers to the buyer for both conforming and nonconforming goods. Title reverts back to seller if when goods are rejected by the buyer.

Risk of Loss

Risk of loss may pass with title or at the time specified by the contract. Risk remains with the seller:

- When nonconforming goods are sent even if shipment contract exists
- Until delivery when the shipper's vessel is used for shipment
- Until delivered to a common carrier in a shipment contract
- Until delivered to their destination by a common carrier in a destination contract

When goods are not delivered

- A merchant seller retains the risk of loss until the buyer has possession of the goods
- A nonmerchant seller transfers the risk of loss when tendering delivery to the buyer

Obligations of Common Carriers

In shipment contract, common carrier is a bailee in a mutual-benefit bailment. Standard of care is based on strict liability

- Responsible for loss regardless of negligence
- Amount of loss is limited by law

Types of Remedies and Formulas for Damage

Breach of Contract

Different remedies are available to buyer and seller for the other party's breach of a sales contract.

Seller's Remedies

When a buyer is in breach, the seller may

- Cancel the contract
- Recover damages

Damages may include

- The contract price of the goods if they cannot be resold
- The difference between the contract price and the sales price if they can be resold
- Incidental damages for costs incurred as a result of the buyer's breach

Punitive damages are not available.

Buyer's Remedies

A seller is in breach by not shipping goods or by shipping nonconforming goods. Nonconforming goods include a combination of conforming and nonconforming goods.

When goods are not shipped, the buyer may

- Obtain specific performance if the goods are unique
- **Cover** the contract by acquiring goods elsewhere and recovering the excess cost from the seller

When nonconforming goods are shipped, the buyer may void the contract. The buyer

- May reject all, some, or none of the goods shipped
- Must notify the seller of the rejection
- Must give the seller an opportunity to cure the defect on a timely basis
- Must follow reasonable instructions from the seller in disposing of rejected goods
- May avoid costs incurred in relation to the rejected goods

When partial payment is made to an insolvent seller, the buyer may recover or capture goods identified to the contract that are in the possession of the seller under the right of **replevin**.

Special Circumstances

Remedies available to the parties may be modified by special circumstances

- When goods are accidentally destroyed before the passing of title, the seller is released from obligation to perform
- When the agreed-upon delivery method becomes impracticable, a practical alternative must be tendered and accepted
- A liquidated damages clause may specify the amount of damages to be received by a party in the case of breach by the other, provided it is reasonable

Sales

Contracts involving the sale or lease of goods are covered by the Uniform Commercial Code and are subject to special rules.

Offer, Acceptance, and Enforceability

Like other contracts, elements of a sales contract include offer, acceptance, and consideration.

Offer

An offer under sales law may be incomplete as to terms provided the parties intend to enter into a contract.

A **firm offer** cannot be revoked for a specified time of up to three months, regardless of a lack of consideration. A firm offer must be

- Made by a merchant
- In a signed writing

Acceptance

Acceptance of a sales contract does not have to mirror the offer. A timely and definite indication of acceptance with different or additional terms is valid.

1) The different or additional terms are generally considered proposals
2) If the contract is between merchants, the different or additional terms are part of the contract unless

   - The offer required acceptance of the specified terms
   - The changes materially change the offer
   - The other party objects on a timely basis

An offer to buy goods for prompt or current shipment

- May be accepted by a promise to ship promptly
- May be accepted by prompt shipment of conforming goods

Enforceability

Modifications of existing contracts are enforceable, even if or not supported by additional consideration.

Under the Statute of Frauds, sales contracts in the amount of $500 or more, including modifications, must be in writing to be enforceable.

- An oral contract between merchants for $500 or more will be enforceable if:
    - There is a written confirmation signed by one party, and
    - The other party fails to make a timely written objection.

Other oral contracts for $500 or more that will be enforceable include

- A contract for specially manufactured goods
- A contracted admitted to by the party
- Portions of a contract that have already been performed

DEBTOR-CREDITOR RELATIONSHIPS

Suretyship: Introduction, Creation, and Types

Types of Sureties

Surety—Party agreeing to answer for debts of another

Cosureties—Two or more parties responsible for the same debt of another

Obligations of Sureties

Guarantees obligation of principal debtor

Immediately liable upon default—Creditor not required to

- Collect from principal debtor
- Use collateral of debtor
- Provide notice of default to surety

Rights of Sureties

Exoneration—Require the principal debtor to pay the obligation

Reimbursement—Obtain repayment from principal debtor

Subrogation—Obtain rights of creditor against debtor and debtor's collateral

Contribution—Receive proportionate payment from cosureties

Defenses of Sureties

Statute of Frauds—A surety contract must be in writing to be enforceable

Capacity—Surety must have capacity to enter into contract

Bankruptcy—A surety can be released in bankruptcy, but is not released due to the principal debtor's bankruptcy

Misrepresentation—Surety is released due to fraudulent misrepresentations of principal debtor known to creditor

Surety is not released from debt obligation even if principal debtor is released from debt obligation

Surety's debt obligation will be reduced if debtor's collateral is released by the creditor without the surety's consent

Cosureties

Obligations of Cosureties

Cosureties are individually liable to the creditor up to the maximum amount that the cosurety guaranteed.

Cosureties may demand a contribution from other cosureties, if a cosurety pays more than its proportionate share of the debt.

To calculate proportionate share of cosureties:

1. Add up total amount guaranteed by all cosureties
2. Divide each individual cosurety's guarantee by the total in 1. above
3. Multiply the resulting percentage and the amount of the defaulted debt
4. The result is that cosurety's proportionate share

If a cosurety is released by the creditor, the remaining sureties are not liable for the proportionate share of the released surety.

SECURED TRANSACTIONS

An agreement where a creditor receives additional assurance of repayment from a debtor who provides collateral in which the creditor obtains an interest:

Collateral

The personal property that is subject to the creditor's security interest

Types of Collateral

Goods

- Consumer goods are goods for personal use
- Equipment is goods used for business
- Inventory is goods used for resale

Indispensible paper

Intangibles

Security Agreement

The agreement between the debtor and creditor that gives the creditor a security interest in the debtor's collateral

Requirements for a valid security agreement

- In writing, except when creditor has physical possession of collateral
- Signed by the debtor
- A description of the collateral

Attachment and Perfection

Attachment

Gives secured creditor right to collateral upon default of debtor

Conditions for attachment—all three must be met

1. Creditor **g**ives value to debtor
2. Debtor has **r**ights **i**n the property
3. Creditor takes **p**ossession of property or obtains written **s**ecurity agreement

   *A security interest attaches to collateral and the creditor **grips** the debtor's property.*

Perfection

Gives secured creditor a claim to the property that is superior to others

Perfection occurs when the secured interest has **at**tached and one of the following:

- A financing **s**tatement has been filed
- A purchase money security interest (PMSI) is perfected **a**utomatically when it attaches in a consumer sale
- The creditor has taken **p**ossession of the property

    *A creditor should perfect a security interest **ASAP** (as soon as possible).*

Priorities Among Claims

A PMSI has highest priority if the creditor fulfills requirements

Requirements for PMSI in noninventory goods to have highest priority

- Must be perfected within twenty days of debtor possessing collateral

Requirements for PMSI in inventory to have highest priority

- Must be perfected prior to debtor receiving inventory
- Written notice must be given to other perfected interests prior to debtor receiving inventory

Among other claims

- If all perfected by filing, in order of filing date
- If perfection by filing versus perfection by possession, in order of perfection date

Priorities Among Claims (continued)

Buyers of Property

- A buyer of goods in the ordinary course of business is not subject to security interest (i.e., the security interest cannot be enforced against a buyer in the ordinary course of business).
- A good-faith buyer of used consumer goods from another consumer takes them free of any security interest except those perfected by filing

Default by Debtor

Repossession by Creditor

- Debtor can exercise right of redemption by paying off loan
- Proceeds from sale of repossessed property are distributed in the following order:
  1. Reasonable expenses of sale
  2. Pay secured party's claim
  3. Satisfy other secured claims in order of priority
  4. Excess to debtor

BANKRUPTCY

Voluntary Filing—Chapter 7

Means testing for consumer debtor added by Bankruptcy Act of 2005, prohibiting Chapter 7 filing when

- Consumer debtor monthly income exceeds certain specified amounts in the bankruptcy code
- Debtor current monthly income is reduced by
  - Monthly expenses
  - Payment made on secured debts, and
  - Payment made to priority general creditors

Consumer debtor must meet with an authorized credit counselor within 180 days prior to filing for bankruptcy

Involuntary Filing—Chapter 7

Twelve or more unsecured creditors

- Requires three or more unsecured creditors to file petition
- Total undisputed claims of petitioners ≥ $15,775

Fewer than twelve unsecured creditors

- Requires only one or more unsecured creditors to file petition
- Total undisputed claims of petitioners ≥ $15,775

Business Reorganizations—Chapter 11

Plan for Repayment

Agreed to by debtor and creditors

Debtor continues to operate business

Debtor or creditor's committee files reorganization plan

- Submitted to each class of creditors
- Must be approved by at least 1/2 of claims
- Total of approving claims ≥ 2/3 of total amount of claims

Court Confirmation of Plan

For confirmation, must provide for payment of priority general creditors:

- Administrative expenses
- Gap creditors
- Employee claims for wages, salaries, and benefits
- Consumer deposits

Upon confirmation, plan is binding on debtor and creditors

Discharge

Debtor discharged from debts arising before confirmation

Exceptions to discharge

- Debts protected under plan
- Debts exempt from discharge under plan of reorganization

Repayment Plans—Chapter 13

Qualifying Debtors

Available to debtors with

- Regular income
- Generally limited to individuals, or small businesses

Debtor's Plan

Provides for

- Debtor's future income controlled by trustee
- Full payment of priority claims
- Similar treatment to all claims within a given class of claims

Plan confirmed by courts

Alternatives to Bankruptcy

Composition of creditors

- Agreement between debtor and certain creditors
- Creditors agree to accept portion of their claims
- Remainder of claims of agreeing creditors discharged

Assignment for the benefit of creditors (general assignment)

- Debtor transfers property to trustee
- Trustee applies property proportionately to debts
- Debtor not discharged from remaining claims

Powers of Bankruptcy Trustee

Avoidance

Enables trustee to obtain return of debtor's property

Applies to

1) **F**raudulent transfers
2) Statutory **l**iens against debtor's property
3) **A**fter-filing date transfers
4) Voidable **p**references

   *His attempt to transfer the property caused a **flap***

Voidable Preferences

Transfers of property made by debtor that can be recovered by trustee

To be a voidable preference, the transfer must be made:

- Within **n**inety days of filing of petition if to a noninsider
- Within **o**ne year of filing if to an insider
- For a **p**re-existing (antecedent) debt
- While the debtor is **i**nsolvent
- When the transfer **e**xceeds the amount that the creditor would obtain through bankruptcy

  *In essence, the transferee gets **no pie** and must return the debtor's property*

Distribution of Assets

Order of Distribution

1) Secured creditors
2) Priority claims
3) Unsecured creditors

Secured Creditors

Fully secured creditors obtain collateral

- When property satisfies debt
- If value of property exceeds debt, then excess is added to bankrupt's estate

Partially secured creditors obtain collateral

- When property does not satisfy debt
- If debt exceeds value of property, then excess debt becomes unsecured claim

Priority Claims

Certain creditors will be paid first, in order of priority

1) Perfected secured parties—Perfected secured parties have priority to the collateral or proceeds over general creditors and the trustee
2) Support payments (including alimony and child support)
3) Trustee fees and administrative expenses of the bankruptcy
4) Obligations created after petition filing by creditors before settlement (i.e., involuntary gap creditors)
5) Payroll arising within 90 days of petition up to $12,850 per employee and contributions to employee benefit plans arising within 180 days up to $12,850
6) Claims of farm producers and fishermen up to a limit per creditor.
7) Individual deposits on consumer goods not received—up to $2,850 per individual
8) Taxes owed to federal, state, and local governments
9) Claims for death or personal injury
10) All general unsecured creditors
11) If any amount is left, it goes to the debtor

Focus on
Bankruptcy

Unsecured Creditors

- Each level of priority claims must be paid in full before the next level of priority claim is paid.
- If there are insufficient assets to pay a level in full, then that level is paid on a pro rata basis. For example, each claim might receive 50 cents for each dollar it is owed.
- Claims below the group paid on a pro rata basis receive nothing.

Exceptions to Discharge

Certain debts are not discharged as a result of bankruptcy

- **S**tudent loans of debtor (Exception if debtor can demonstrate undue hardship)
- **T**axes accruing within three years of the bankruptcy (Taxes can be discharged if they came due 3 years before filing for bankruptcy, as long as it has been at least 2 years since filing the tax forms and 240 days since the taxes were assessed.)
- **U**nscheduled debt causing credit not to be notified of bankruptcy
- **P**ension and profit sharing obligations to employees
- **I**ntentional force or fraud against another person
- **D**omestic support obligations for alimony and child support

> *A debtor is **stupid** if he thinks he can use bankruptcy to get these debts discharged.*

Denial of Discharge

Court may deny discharge of all unpaid debts in limited circumstances

- **B**ankruptcy offense, such as hiding assets from the bankruptcy trustees, committed by debtor
- **A**ctive operations continue for partnership, corporation, or any business entity
- **D**ischarge previously obtained within past eight years

  *A court will completely deny a debtor any discharge for **bad** behavior.*

FEDERAL SECURITIES REGULATION

Securities Act of 1933 (33 Act)

The 33 Act requires

- Registration of securities offered for sale to the public
- Information be provided as part of that registration

Nonexempt securities must be registered before being offered for sale to the public

- Through the mails
- In interstate commerce

Registration consists of a registration statement, which includes the prospectus

- The **registration statement** describes the use of proceeds and contains audited financial statements
- The **prospectus** describes the securities, the company, and the risk

33 Act (continued)

Once registration statement is filed

1) Oral offers to sell shares may be made
2) 20 day waiting period before registration is effective
3) During waiting period company may obtain an underwriter and issue a "red herring" (preliminary prospectus)
4) After waiting period, securities can be bought and sold
5) After waiting period, a **tombstone ad** informs investors about obtaining prospectus

In addition to federal registration laws, states require registration under "**blue-sky laws**"

Exempt Transactions and Securities

Securities Exempt from Registration

Certain securities are exempt from registration. The 1933 Act doesn't apply to these securities at all.

Exempt securities include

- Government securities
- Regulated by federal agency (banks and railroads)
- Insurance policy
- Nonprofit organization
- Debt maturing within 9 months (known as commercial paper)

Transactions Exempt from Registration

Certain transactions may qualify for exemption from registration. The securities themselves remain subject to the 1933 Act for other purposes or subsequent transactions that aren't exempt.

Exempt transactions include

- Splits, dividends, and other exchanges with existing shareholders without charge
- Casual sales by parties other than issuers, underwriters, dealers, directors, officers, or 10% or greater shareholders
- Intrastate offers (as long as shares aren't resold to nonresidents for 9 months)
- Private placements under Regulation D
- Small issues under Regulation A

Transactions Exempt from Registration (continued)

	Reg A	Reg D Rule 506	Reg D Rule 505	Reg D Rule 504
Maximum $ amount	$20,000,000 tier 1; $50,000,000 tier 2	No limit	$5,000,000	$1,000,000
Time to complete offering	12 mo.	No limit	12 mo	12 mo
Accredited Investors	None tier 1; Nonaccredited investors have a 10% limit	No max	No max	No max
Nonaccredited Investors		35	35	No max
Filing requirements	Offering circular	Form D	Form D	Form D
Resale restricted	None	1 year	1 year	1 year
General advertising/ solicitation allowed	Testing the waters provision	Generally okay if selling only to accredited investors	Generally okay if selling only to accredited investors	Generally okay if selling only to accredited investors

Emerging Growth Companies (EGCs)

The JOBS Act of 2012 is a securities law that amended federal law with the goal of making it easier for small companies to raise capital and the hope that this would eventually lead to job creation. The JOBS Act allows relatively small firms to declare themselves EGCs and go public but delay complying with all the regulatory burdens for a period of five years (e.g., having an audit of internal controls). To be an EGC, a firm must meet the following criteria:

- Have less than $1 billion in annual gross revenues during its most recently completed fiscal year,
- Have been publicly traded for less than five years,
- Have a public float of less than $700 million, and
- Have not issued $1 billion in non-convertible debt in the prior three-year period.

Securities Exchange Act of 1934 (34 Act)

The 34 Act established the SEC and made it responsible for

- Requiring disclosures concerning offerings on national securities exchanges
- Regulating activities of securities brokers
- Investigating securities fraud

Companies are required to file periodic reports if

- Company's securities are traded on securities exchanges
- Company's assets > $10,000,000 and more than 500 unaccredited shareholders or 2,000 or more total shareholders (This does not include shares obtained from a qualified employee compensation plan)

Registration

Information required upon registration

- Financial structure and nature of business
- Names of officers and directors
- Disclosure of bonus and profit-sharing arrangements

Reporting

Required reports include

- 10-K (annual report)—includes audited financial statements
- 10-Q and 8-K (periodic reports)—update information in original registration

Proxies

Shareholders may sign proxies authorizing the company to vote their shares. The company must file a preliminary copy of the proxy statement with the SEC at least 10 days before it is sent to shareholders.

Insider Trading

Insider trading must be reported to the SEC.

- Insiders include agents of the issuer, such as attorneys, or directors, officers, and owners of 10% or more of any class of stock
- Short swing profits must be returned to the company

Liability under 34 Act

Accountants are liable under Rule 10b-5 of the 34 Act:

- Liable for oral or written misrepresentations of fact
- Liable for wrongful act committed through mail, interstate commerce, or a national securities exchange

To be successful, the plaintiff must prove:

- Scienter
- Reliance

Defenses the accountant may use include:

- Plaintiff's knowledge of the error
- Lack of reliance by plaintiff

Summary of Auditor Liability

Elements in action taken against an accountant

1) There is a misstatement or omission of a material fact
2) Plaintiff has reasonably relied upon the information
3) Plaintiff suffered a loss
4) Accountant was in error

Auditor Common Law Liability

	Contracts	Negligence	Gross Negligence or Fraud
Who may bring action	Client or an intended user	Client or (usually) foreseen user	Anyone injured
Accountant's error resulting in action	Breach of contract	Carelessness	Recklessness or intentional misconduct (scienter)
Plaintiff must prove	All four elements	All four elements	All four elements

Auditor Liability under Federal Securities Laws

	1933 Act Section 11	1934 Act Rule 10b-5
Who may bring action	Any purchaser	Any purchaser
Accountant's error resulting in action	Lack of due diligence	Recklessness or intentional misconduct (scienter)
Plaintiff must prove	Elements 1 and 3 only	All four elements

FICA AND FUTA

Federal Insurance Contributions Act (FICA)

The Social Security Act provides for

- Old age or retirement benefits
- Benefits to survivors and divorced spouses
- Payments for disability and to disabled children
- Medicare benefits

Benefits are paid for by contributions by employer and amounts withheld from employee. If an employer fails to withhold

- The employer must pay the employee's share
- The employer may be reimbursed by the employee
- Unreimbursed amounts are compensation to the employee

Self-employed individuals must pay both the employer and the employee's share.

Federal Unemployment Tax Act (FUTA)

FUTA provides compensation to employees losing their jobs

- Applies in the case of business reversals
- Does not apply to terminations for cause
- Does not apply to employees leaving voluntarily or refusing reasonable employment after losing their jobs

FUTA taxes are paid by employers

- Not all employers are subject to FUTA
- Amounts paid for state unemployment taxes reduce required FUTA payments

Federal Insurance Contributions Act (FICA) (continued)

Employer and employees pay payroll taxes. FICA tax rate of 15.3% consists of the Medicare tax rate and the Social Security tax rate.

- Medicare tax of 1.45% paid by both employee and employer on 100% of wages
- The employee portion of Medicare tax is increased by 0.9% for wages in excess of $200,000 ($250,000 on a joint return, $125,000 for married filing separately)
- FICA tax rate also includes 6.2% paid by both employee and employer on wages up to a base amount ($127,200 for 2017) for Social Security.

Self-employed individuals pay employer's and employee's shares

- Net earnings from self-employment × 15.3% = Self-employment tax
- Full self-employment tax capped at $127,200; the Medicare portion is not capped
- The Medicare tax is increased by 0.9% for net earnings from self-employment in excess of $200,000 ($250,000 on a joint return, $125,000 for married filing separately)
- 50% of self-employment tax is deduction for AGI

BUSINESS STRUCTURE

Selection and Formation of a Business Entity

Partnership Characteristics

Partners' Rights

1) Participation in management
2) Sharing of profits and losses

   - Percentages may be specified in partnership agreement
   - Equal sharing of profits and losses when not specified
   - If profits are allocated, but losses are not, then losses will be allocated the same as profits

3) Property rights

Partners' Property Rights

Partner's interest; this is only a partner's right to profits

- Right to share of profits and capital upon termination
- May be sold or assigned
- Buyer or assignee does not have same rights as partner

Right to specific property

- Partnership purposes only
- Individual partners may not sell or assign

Partners' Authority

Authority to bind partnership and other partners

- Actual authority—express or implied
- Apparent authority—reasonable third party would believe partner has authority

Individual partner does **not** have apparent authority to

- Admit a new partner
- Guarantee debts of a third party
- Admit a claim in court or submit a legal claim to binding arbitration
- Sell or pledge partnership property (other than ordinary sales of inventory)

Partner has apparent authority for any other action that appears to be in the course of partnership business unless **both** of the following occur

- Partners mutually agree on a limit to the authority
- Third parties are notified of this limit

Partners' Liability

Jointly and severally liable

- Liable for debts of partnership and torts committed by other partners engaged in partnership business
- Right of contribution from other partners
- Creditor must attempt to collect from partnership before partners unless partnership in bankruptcy

Notice is required after a partner dissociates from the partnership to avoid liability for later actions

- Personal notice to third parties who dealt with the partner (actual notice)
- Public notice for all others (constructive notice)
- A statement of dissociation, filed with the state's secretary of state, will provide notice 90 days after it is filed

Liability of Entering and Exiting Partners

Entering partner

- Not personally liable for debts created before entering, but may lose capital contributed to partnership
- Personally liable for all debts created after entering

Exiting partner

- Liable for all debts created prior to exiting unless creditors perform a novation to release the exiting partner
- Not liable for debts created after exiting as long as proper notice has been given to third parties of the exit

Formation of Partnership

Creation of partnership does not require government approval, and is created by agreement

- Written—When a partnership falls within the Statute of Frauds (such as when partners agree that the term of the partnership will exceed one year), the partnership agreement must be in writing and signed by all parties.
- Oral—In other circumstances, an oral agreement will be sufficient.
- Implied—Even in the absence of a written or oral agreement, if two or more people are sharing the profits from a venture, there is legal presumption that they are partners unless they can demonstrate otherwise.

Partnership Dissolution

Partnership does **not** automatically dissolve upon

- Withdrawal of a partner
- Death or bankruptcy of a partner

Partnership Dissolution (continued)

Remaining partners with majority vote may continue partnership

- Individual partners have right to withdraw
- Withdrawing partner may be in breach of contract

Distributions upon liquidation

- 1st to creditors for loans
- 2nd to partners for capital contributions
- 3rd any remainder is given to partners as profits

Limited Liability Arrangements

Limited Partnerships

Basic requirements

- At least one general partner with unlimited liability
- At least one limited partner
- Must file certificate with the state that contains the names of all general partners

Status of limited partners

- Have right to profits but not to participation in management or use of property
- Limited partner who participates in management or uses property loses limited liability protection

Limited Liability Partnerships (LLPs)

Partners have unique status under this arrangement

- All partners may participate in management
- Partners are personally liable for own negligence, malpractice, or fraud
- Partners are liable for negligence, malpractice by employees/partners under their immediate supervision
- Partners are **not** liable for negligence, malpractice, or fraud committed by other partners
- Taxed as partnership (income and losses passed through to individual returns of partners)
- Form of organization common in many licensed professions (accountants, attorneys)

Limited Liability Companies (LLCs)

Characteristics of corporations and partnerships

- Limited liability to all members
- All members may participate in management
- Multiple member LLC taxed as partnership (unless members elect to be taxed as corporation)
- Single member LLC taxed as sole proprietorship

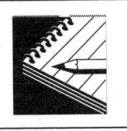

Corporations

Characteristics of Corporations

Corporations are legal entities, separate from their owners

- They are generally taxed on their own income
- Shareholders are taxed only on distributed income
- Shareholders are not liable for corporate obligations

Corporations are incorporated by the various states

- Domestic—A corporation that is operating within the state of incorporation
- Foreign—A corporation when it is operating in a different state
- Alien—A corporation when it is operating in a different country

Foreign and alien corporations must obtain approval to operate in the other state, or they will not have the protection of its courts and be subject to fines (as well as the normal taxes and fees that would have been owed had they qualified to operate in that state)

Focus on
Business Structure

S Corporations

S corporations provide liability protection to shareholders, but are not taxed on their own income.

- Corporate income passes through and is taxed to the shareholders
- Shareholders are not taxed on distributions

Requirements for S corporations

- Domestic corporation
- Not member of affiliated group
- 100 or fewer shareholders
- Only one class of stock
- Shareholders generally need to be individuals and United States residents

Articles of Incorporation

Primary document in process of incorporation Includes:

- Name of corporation
- Capital structure
- Name and address of registered agent
- Name and address of each incorporator
- Corporate purpose

State issues certificate of incorporation or corporate charter

- Incorporators elect board of directors
- Board of directors adopts initial bylaws

Promoters

Prior to the formation of a corporation, promoters may act on behalf of proposed corporation

- They do not have status of agents, as no principal exists to give them authority
- Contracts made on behalf of corporation bind promoter instead
- Promoter still has fiduciary duty to proposed corporation to act loyally and in good faith
- Board of directors may adopt or reject contracts previously made by promoter
- Promoters remain liable to other party to contract unless granted a novation by them
- Promoters have no special right to compensation for services rendered before corporation has been formed

Directors and Officers

Shareholders elect directors, who

- Set corporate policy
- Select officers
- May terminate officers

Rights of Directors

Directors' rights include

- Notification of meetings
- Participation in oversight of company
- Access to books and records

In addition, directors may receive

- Compensation
- Indemnification in the form of reimbursement of losses incurred in corporation-related lawsuits

Powers of the Board of Directors

Board, not individual directors, is an agent of the corporation

- Acts as a single body—Individual directors are **not** agents and may not act alone
- Hires, fires, and sets salaries of officers
- Issues stock to buyers at mutually agreed prices
- Board may also repurchase shares and retire them or hold them as **treasury shares**
- Board sets dividend policy, determining if there are sufficient resources to pay a dividend that year and setting the amount of the dividend
- Dividends may not be declared if the corporation is insolvent or will be made so by dividend
- Dividends that exceed retained earnings require shareholder approval

Rights of Officers

Officers are selected and supervised by directors who also set their compensation. Officers are responsible for the day-to-day operations of the corporation. An officer

- May be a director and may be a stockholder
- Is an agent of the corporation as an officer
- May be entitled to indemnification

Duties of Directors and Officers

Directors and officers have a fiduciary responsibility to the corporation and owe it the duties of care and loyalty.

- Care—They must act honestly and prudently when conducting corporate affairs
- Loyalty—They must subordinate personal interests to those of the corporation

The duty of loyalty prohibits

- Competing with the corporation
- Using corporate opportunities for personal gain
- Having interests in conflict with the corporation's
- Trading based on inside information
- Authorizing transactions detrimental to minority shareholders
- Selling control over the corporation

PROPERTY TRANSACTIONS

Realized Gain or Loss

Amount realized

-   Adjusted basis
- =   Realized gain or loss

Amount Realized

Cash received

- +   FMV of property received
- +   Net debt relief
- –   Direct selling expenses
- =   Amount realized

Net debt relief = Liabilities transferred – Liabilities assumed

Adjusted Basis

Initial basis
+ Improvements
− Depreciation
− Costs recovered
± Adjustments
= Adjusted basis

Initial Basis

Property converted from personal use to business or investment use	Lower of actual basis or FMV on date of conversion
Inherited property	FMV at date of death or alternate valuation date (date of distribution up to six months after death)
Property received as gift	Gain = Same as donor's basis (transferred basis) Loss = Lesser of (a) gain basis, or (FMV) at date of gift

Taxation of Gains and Losses

	Tax Treatment
Ordinary assets • Inventory • Business receivables • Self-created artistic works • Business assets held ≤ year	Regular rates
Section 1231 assets (business assets held > year) • Depreciable or amortizable business assets • Land used in business	Net gain—generally treated as LTCG Net loss—ordinary loss deduction

Capital assets all others	INDIVIDUALS LTCG—Reduced rates
	   STCG—Regular rates
	   Net loss – Max of $3,000 during current year
	   Carryforward indefinite
	CORPORATIONS
	   Net loss—not deductible
	   Carryback 3 and carryforward 5 years as STCL

Focus on

Property Transactions

97

Related-Taxpayer Transactions

Related taxpayers include

- Taxpayer's spouse, brothers, sisters, ancestors (parent, grandparent, etc.), lineal descendants (child, grandchild, etc.)
- Corporation or partnership where direct or constructive ownership > 50%

Tax effects

- Losses—not deductible by seller
- Buyer's basis—purchase price
- Buyer's subsequent gain on sales—taxed to extent subsequent gain > nondeductible loss

Special Transactions

Type of Transaction	Special Rule
Sale of personal assets	Gain recognized as capital gain; losses are not deductible
Wash sales—Taxpayer acquires same stock or securities within 30 days before or after selling stock or securities at a loss	Loss not recognized, but added to basis of new stock or securities
Related-party transactions	Losses not recognized
Like-kind exchanges	Losses not recognized Gains recognized to extent of boot received
Involuntary conversions Replacement property acquired within two years of end of year in which gain realized for casualty or theft, three years for condemnation	If cost of replacement property ≥ proceeds—no gain recognized If cost of replacement property < proceeds—gain recognized = proceeds − cost or replacement property

Special Transactions (continued)

Type of Transaction	Special Rule
Installment sale	Gain recognized: Gross profit × Amount received in year ÷ Total sales price
Sale of principal residence If taxpayer owned and lived in home at least two of the five years preceding sale	Up to $250,000 of gain excluded ($500,000 for married filing jointly). Gain in excess of exclusion is recognized as capital gain. Excluded gain does not affect basis of new residence.

Sec. 1245 Depreciation Recapture

Applies to the disposition of depreciable personal property (e.g., trucks, autos, machinery, equipment)

Realized gain

  − Depreciation recapture (treated as ordinary income)

  = Section 1231 gain

Amount of depreciation recapture

- Realized gain < accumulated depreciation, use amount of gain
- Realized gain ≥ accumulated depreciation, use accumulated depreciation

INDIVIDUAL TAXATION

Individual Income Tax

Computing Individual Income Tax

Gross income

-     Adjustments

=   Adjusted gross income (AGI)

-     Greater of standard deduction or itemized deductions

-     Exemptions

=   Taxable income

×   Tax rate

=   Tentative tax amount

-     Credits

+   Self-employment tax

Individual Income Tax (Continued)

+   Alternative minimum tax

=   Total tax

−   Prepayments

=   Tax due or refund amount

Gross Income—Other Inclusions

Compensation for Services

Included

- Wages, salaries, and tips
- Bonuses and commissions
- Fees for jury duty
- Discounts on purchases of employer's merchandise to the extent in excess of gross profit percentage
- Taxable fringe benefits such as use of company vehicle for personal purposes

Excluded

- Health insurance paid by employer
- Cost of group term life insurance up to $50,000 in coverage
- Employer-provided educational assistance (limited to $5,250)
- Fringe benefits incurred for employer's benefit, such as housing provided to on-site hotel manager

Gross Income—Other Inclusions (continued)

Prizes and Awards

Generally taxable

Excluded from income if an employee achievement award of tangible personal property received from employer for years of employment or safety achievement

Interest

Included in income

- Interest received or credited to taxpayer
- Interest accrued on zero-coupon bond
- Amortization of bond discount
- Interest on US Treasury obligations
- Interest on tax refunds and insurance policies
- Interest portion of annuities received
- Interest on Series HH US savings bonds

Excluded from income

- Interest on state and municipal bonds
- Interest on series EE bonds if the redemption proceeds are used to finance the higher education of the taxpayer, spouse, or dependents

Other Income

Additional items *included* in gross income

- Rents and royalties including rent collected in advance and nonrefundable deposits
- Discount on nonqualified stock option upon exercise
- Injury awards for punitive damages or lost profits
- Up to 85% of social security benefits may be included if the taxpayer's provisional income (PI) exceeds a specified amount,
- State tax refunds if originally claimed as an itemized deduction
- Proceeds from a traditional IRA of contributions previously deducted
- Proceeds from a traditional IRA representing earnings of IRA
- Alimony received in cash provided the payments will terminate upon recipient's death
- Unemployment compensation
- Flow-through entity ordinary business income

Other Income

Additional items *excluded* from gross income

- Damages received for physical injury or lost wages
- Workers' compensation benefits
- Social Security received by low-income taxpayers
- Portion of traditional IRA or pension withdrawal of prior nondeductible contributions
- Qualified Roth IRA withdrawals
- Federal tax refunds
- Gifts and inheritances
- Life insurance proceeds paid by reason of death
- Divorce property settlements
- Child support payments
- Discharge of qualified principal residence indebtedness (expired 12/31/16)

Taxation of Income from Business Entities

Dividends

Generally included in gross income

- Ordinary income distributions from real estate investment trusts (REITs) are taxed as ordinary income
- Capital gain distributions from REITs are taxed as long-term capital gains

Excluded from income

- Nontaxable stock dividends
- Distributions received from an S corporation
- Dividends received on a life insurance policy
- Dividends received from mutual funds investing in tax-exempt bonds

Dividends (continued)

Special favorable tax rates available for qualified dividends

- Tax rate 15% for most taxpayers, 20% if ordinary rate would otherwise be 39.6%
- Tax rate 0% if ordinary rate would otherwise be 10% or 15%
- Stock on which the dividend is paid must be held for > 60 days during the 121-day period beginning 60 days before the ex-dividend date
- Available for distributions from mutual funds only to extent mutual fund received dividends from taxable corporations
- Available for dividends from foreign corporations traded on US stock exchanges

Special rate not available for some dividends

- Distributions from REITs
- Distributions from partnerships and S corporations
- Mutual fund dividends that represent interest income (such as from bond funds)

Business Expenses (Schedule C)

Include all reasonable business expenses

- Employee wages and payroll taxes
- Contributions to employee retirement plans
- Employee fringe benefits
- Interest on business loans
- Business taxes
- Casualty losses on business property
- 50% of business meals and entertainment
- Bad debts when accounts are written off (generally no deduction for cash method taxpayers)
- Gifts to customers and clients up to $25 per recipient per year

A net business loss reduces wages and business income, including net rental income, with any excess carried back or forward.

Rent and Royalty Expenses (Schedule E)

Expenses incurred on property generating rent or royalty income reduce the amount of rent or royalty income reported on Schedule E and include

- Depreciation or amortization
- Mortgage interest
- Property taxes
- Insurance and maintenance

Rental and royalty properties are generally considered passive activities

- Any activity in which the investor does not materially participate
- Any real estate rental activity

Rent and Royalty Expenses (Schedule E) (continued)

Passive activity losses are not generally deductible

- Investor actively managing real estate rental property with AGI below $100,000 may deduct up to $25,000 per year (reduced by 50% of AGI > $100,000)
- Real estate broker or developer may deduct real estate losses if eligibility requirements met
- Nondeductible passive activity losses may be carried forward indefinitely or deducted when property sold

Deductions for AGI

Items that may be deducted as adjustments for AGI include

- **I**nterest on student loans
- **E**mployment tax—50% of self-employment tax paid
- **M**oving expense
- **B**usiness owner health insurance premiums for self and family
- **R**etirement plan contributions
- **A**limony paid
- **C**ollege tuition and fees (unless American Opportunity or Lifetime Learning Credit claimed) (expired 12/31/16)
- **E**arly withdrawal penalties on time deposits

 I EMBRACE adjustments that reduce AGI and lower taxes

Moving Expenses

Moving expenses are deducted if three conditions are met

- Taxpayer moved due to change in location of job or business
- Taxpayer remains employed for at least 39 weeks after the move
- Commute from old residence to new job at least 50 miles longer than commute from old residence to old job

Amounts deductible include direct costs of moving family and belongings

- Airfares
- Shipping and temporary storage
- Cost of traveling (including lodging) and transportation to new location (auto depreciation, gas, repairs), or standard mileage rate

Contributions to Retirement Plans

Amounts deducted for contributions to retirement plans are subject to limitations.

- A self-employed individual may deduct contributions to a defined-contribution self-employed retirement plan up to the lesser of $54,000, or 100% of earned (for 2017)
- An employee may exclude contributions (up to specified amount) contributed to a 401(k) plan
- A taxpayer may deduct up to $5,500 for 2017 (plus additional $1,000 if 50 or over) contributed to a traditional IRA, not to exceed earned income
- A married couple may deduct contributions to an IRA for each spouse, even though only one spouse has earned income

In order to deduct traditional IRA contributions, taxpayer must

- Not participate in a qualified pension or profit-sharing plan at work, and
- Have adjusted gross income below a specified level

Roth IRAs

Individuals may contribute to a **Roth IRA** instead of a traditional IRA

- Not available to taxpayers with very high AGI
- Subject to same contribution limitation as traditional IRA
- Contributions are not deductible
- Neither contributions nor earnings subject to income tax when withdrawn

Withdrawn earnings are not taxable provided

- Taxpayer is a least 59½ years old
- Taxpayer is disabled, deceased, or using withdrawal for first home purchase

Coverdell Education Savings Accounts (ESAs)

Taxpayer may establish **ESA**

- Not available to taxpayers with very high AGI
- May contribute up to $2,000 annually for each qualified beneficiary
- Must be on behalf of beneficiary under age 18
- Contributions not deductible
- Distributions not taxable if used for qualified higher education expenses

Additional for AGI Deductions

Penalties paid for early withdrawal, such as cashing a certificate of deposit before maturity, reduce AGI

Employees may be entitled to a **jury duty deduction**

- Applies when employer pays regular salary to employee during jury duty
- Employee recognizes both salary and jury duty fees as income
- Portion of jury duty fees remitted to employer are deducted in calculating AGI

Domestic production activities deduction

Standard Deduction

Basic standard deduction depends on filing status

Additional standard deduction allowed when

- Taxpayer is 65 or older
- Spouse is 65 or older
- Taxpayer is blind
- Spouse is blind

Deduction will be greater of available standard deduction or total of itemized deductions.

Itemized Deductions

Itemized deductions include amounts paid for

- **C**ontributions
- **O**ther deductions
- **M**edical expenses subject to 10% of AGI threshold
- **M**iscellaneous expenses subject to 2% of AGI threshold
- **I**nterest
- **T**axes
- **T**heft or casualty losses

*Most taxpayers are **committed** to deducting the maximum amount allowed*

Medical Expenses

Deductible medical expenses include

- Fees to doctors, hospitals, and other providers of medical care
- Amounts paid for prescription drugs
- Premiums for health insurance coverage
- Transportation to doctor, hospital, or other provider

The deduction is reduced by

- Reimbursements received or to be received from insurance
- 10% of AGI for 2017
- Medical expense deduction floor for individuals age 65 and older increases to 10%

Interest Expense

Deductible interest includes interest on home mortgage loans on first or second home

- Loans to buy, build, or improve the home up to $1,000,000
- Loans on home equity up to $100,000
- Loans on second homes are included provided the total falls within the limitations
- Premiums for mortgage insurance deductible as qualified residence interest (expired 12/31/16)

Interest on personal indebtedness is not deductible

- Car loans
- Credit card debt

Taxes

Deductible taxes include

- State and local income taxes (sales taxes may be claimed instead if higher)
- Real property taxes
- Personal property taxes (including vehicle fees that are based on FMV)
- Foreign taxes paid, unless foreign tax credit is elected

Certain taxes are not deductible.

- Inheritance tax
- Federal taxes, including federal income tax and FICA
- Fines
- Licensing and vehicle registration fees (unless based on FMV of vehicle)

Contributions

Charitable contributions are deductible in the period

- Payment is made to a qualified charity
- Property is given to a qualified charity
- Payment to a qualified charity is charged to a credit card

The amount of the deduction includes

- Cash contributions
- Property at FMV if contribution of capital gain property
- Costs incurred in assisting the charity

The deduction does not include

- The value of services performed
- The value of goods or services received in return for a contribution

The deduction is limited

- Maximum deduction = 50% of AGI (30% if appreciated capital gain property)
- Nondeductible amounts may be carried forward up to five years

Casualty or Theft Losses

Amount deductible based on decline in value of property as a result of theft or casualty

- May not exceed adjusted basis for property
- Must result from an identifiable event rather than a gradual decline in value

Each loss is reduced by

- Insurance reimbursements received or expected
- $100 floor

Total losses for the year are further reduced by

- 10% of AGI

If NOL results from casualty and theft losses, can carry back three years instead of normal two years.

Miscellaneous Expenses

Deductible miscellaneous expenses include

- Employee business expenses
- Investment expenses
- Tax preparation fees

Employee business expenses include reasonable unreimbursed costs such as

- Union or professional dues
- Trade journals
- Transportation to clients or customers
- Costs incurred on business trips including airfare, hotel, taxi, telephone, and 50% of business meals and entertainment
- Uniforms
- Depreciation on business assets owned by employee
- Continuing education required to maintain employment

Miscellaneous Expenses (continued)

Employee business expenses do not include commuting to work or education obtained to qualify for new occupation (such as a CPA review course)

Deductible **investment expenses** include

- Safe-deposit box rent
- Subscriptions to investment periodicals
- Fees paid to financial advisors
- Cost of collecting income

Total miscellaneous expenses are reduced by 2% of AGI

Other Itemized Deductions

Additional items may be claimed as itemized deductions, including

- Gambling losses to the extent of winnings included in AGI
- Estate taxes on income in respect of a decedent

Amortization of bond premium

Personal and Dependency Exemptions

Taxpayers may deduct personal exemptions and exemptions for dependents ($4,050 each for 2017)

Personal Exemptions

A taxpayer may claim a personal exemption as a reduction of taxable income

- A married couple may take one exemption for each spouse on a joint return
- An individual who is a dependent on someone else's tax return may not claim a personal exemption

Dependency Exemptions

Dependency requirements

- Must be US citizen, or resident of US, Canada, or Mexico
- Must not file joint return with spouse
- Exception—no tax liability would exist for either spouse on separate returns
- Must be **qualifying child** or **qualifying relative** of taxpayer

Qualifying Child must satisfy four additional requirements

- Relationship—Taxpayer's child, stepchild, sibling (or a descendent of any of these individuals)
- Age—Child must be under age 19, or under 24 and full-time student
- Support—Child must not provide more than half of own support
- Housing—Child must live with taxpayer for more than half of year

Dependency Exemptions (continued)

Qualifying Relative—Must satisfy four additional requirements

- Must not be qualifying child
- Related to taxpayer (closer than cousin), or live in taxpayer's household for entire year (exceptions include birth, death, illness, education, military service)
- Support—Taxpayer must provide more than half of dependent's support
- Gross income—Dependent's gross income must be less than amount of exemption ($4,050 for 2017)

Filing Status

A taxpayer's filing status will determine the rates and various amounts used in computing taxable income and the tax liability

Married Couples

Choice of two alternatives

1. Married, filing jointly
2. Married, filing separately

Must be married as of last day of year or date of death if one spouse died during the year

Unmarried Individuals

One of three alternatives

1) Qualified widow or widower
   - Must be providing > half the costs of maintaining household for dependent child
   - Available for two years after death of spouse
   - Joint return was filed for year of spouse's death
2) Head of household
   - Generally must provide > half of costs of maintaining household for qualifying child or dependent relative living in the same home as taxpayer for more than ½ of year
   - Taxpayer's parent need not live in same home if taxpayer maintains parent's household and parent qualifies as taxpayer's dependent
3) Single—all others

Alternative Minimum Tax (AMT)

Taxable income

±   Adjustments and preferences

=   Alternative minimum taxable income (AMTI)

−   Exemption

=   Base

×   Tax rate

=   Tentative minimum tax

−   Regular tax liability

=   AMT

AMT (continued)

The primary adjustments to income in calculating AMTI are

- **S**tandard deduction
- **I**nterest on home equity loans
- **M**edical expenses subject to 10% of AGI limitation
- **P**ersonal and dependency exemptions
- **L**ocal and state tax deductions
- **E**mployee and investment expenses subject to the 2% of AGI rule

The primary preferences are

- **P**rivate activity bond interest
- **I**ncentive stock options
- **E**xcess depreciation

It's as SIMPLE as PIE to remember the adjustments and preferences for AMTI.

AMT (continued)

AMTI is reduced by the **exemption** amount (varies based on filing status)

- $84,500 for joint filers
- $54,300 for individuals
- $42,250 married filing separately

Resulting base amount × Tax rate = Tentative minimum tax

- 26% × first $187,800 (or $93,900 for married filing separately)
- 28% × (Base amount − $187,800)

Tentative minimum tax − Regular income tax = AMT

- If tentative minimum tax > regular income tax = difference increases tax amount
- If tentative minimum tax < regular income tax = no AMT

AMT paid is allowed as a credit (minimum tax credit) that can be carried forward to reduce future regular tax liability

Medicare Contribution Tax on Net Investment Income

For 2017, tax is 3.8% on lesser of (1) net investment income, or (2) modified AGI in excess of $200,000 ($250,000 for married filing jointly, $125,000 for married filing separately)

Tax Payments

Tax payments include

- Excess payroll taxes withheld
- Federal income taxes withheld
- Estimated tax payments

Excess Payroll Taxes

Employees with two or more employers

- Total wages may exceed base amount for FICA ($127,200 for 2017)
- Maximum FICA = Base amount × FICA rate
- Excess withheld treated as tax payment

Personal Tax Credits

Several credits may reduce a taxpayer's total tax

- Dependent care credit
- Credit for the elderly and disabled
- Earned income credit
- Child tax credit
- American Opportunity and Lifetime Learning Credits
- Foreign tax credit

Earned Income Credit

To qualify, taxpayer must meet two conditions

- Taxpayer has earned income
- Taxpayer maintains a household for more than half the year for a qualifying child

The earned income credit is refundable

- Treated as if paid
- Results in refund if credit exceeds tax liability

Credit for Elderly or Disabled

Allowed for individuals with low income who are over 65 or permanently disabled

Dependent Care Credit

A credit is allowed for

- Generally 20% × amounts paid to care for a qualifying dependent
- Maximum payments eligible for credit = $3,000 for one dependent, $6,000 for two or more dependents
- Taxpayers with AGI ≤ $15,000 may take credit of 35% (reduced by 1% for each $2,000 above AGI of $15,000 until reduced to 20% at AGI of $43,000)

Dependent must be either

- Qualifying child under age 13
- Disabled spouse or disabled dependent of any age

Child Tax Credit

May be claimed for each child under 17

Credit $1,000 per child, but reduced for high-income taxpayers

American Opportunity Credit (Modified HOPE Credit)

May be claimed for first four years of postsecondary education

Credit equals 100% of first $2,000 of tuition and fees plus 25% of next $2,000

Maximum credit $2,500 per qualified family member

Lifetime Learning Credit

May be claimed for tuition and fees not eligible for American Opportunity Credit

Credit equals 20% of first $10,000 of tuition and fees

Maximum credit $2,000 per family

Accounting Method

Individuals generally use the **cash method**—Not allowed for

- Accounting for purchase and sales of inventory
- C corporations or partnerships with a C corporation partner
- Tax shelters
- Business with average gross receipts > $5,000,000

Income is reported when

- Cash is received
- Property is received
- Taxpayer receives an unrestricted right to cash or property (constructive receipt)

Expenses are deducted when

- Cash is paid
- A check is disbursed
- An expense is charged to a credit card

Depreciation

Depreciable Real Property

Depreciable real property is Section 1250 property, subject to the following rules:

Recovery Period

27.5 years for residential real property

39 years for nonresidential real property

Depreciation Method

Depreciation calculated using straight-line method

Mid-month Convention

Year of purchase and year of sale

- Assumed purchased or sold in middle of month of transaction
- ½ month's depreciation taken regardless of date of transaction

Depreciable Personal Property

Depreciable personal property is Section 1245 property, subject to the following rules

Recovery Period

Determined by class of asset

- Equipment, office furniture and fixtures—seven years
- Cars, light trucks, computers, and office equipment—five years
- Small tools—three years

Depreciation Method

General MACRS method is 200% declining balance method, but taxpayer may elect to use either of two other methods

- 150% declining balance method (class-by-class election)
- Straight-line method using the alternative depreciation system (ADS)

Half-Year Convention

Generally required

- Assumes assets acquired or sold in middle of tax year
- Half-year's depreciation taken in year of acquisition and in year of sale

Mid-Quarter Convention

Must be used if > 40% of all personal property placed in service during last three months of tax year

- Assumes assets acquired or sold in middle of quarter in which transaction occurs
- Results in 1/8 of annual deduction if property placed in service during last quarter of year

Section 179 Expense Election

Annual election to treat the cost of qualifying property as expense instead of capital expenditure

- Applies to new or used tangible personal property purchased for use in a business
- Deductible up to lower of net business earnings or $510,000 for 2017
- Reduced dollar-for-dollar by cost of property acquired in excess of $2,030,000 for 2017
- Amount deducted reduces depreciable basis of assets

> ***Example*** *—Company purchases $910,000 of used business equipment during September (assume no other property purchases during year). Taxpayer wants to claim maximum deduction*
>
> *Section 179 Election—$510,000 deduction (maximum allowed)*
>
> *Regular MACRS Depreciation—$57,143 ($400,000 basis after Section 179 deduction x 2/7 DDB x ½ year)*
>
> *Total Deduction is $567,143 ($510,000 + $57,143)*

Estate and Gift Tax

Total taxable gifts during lifetime
+ Total taxable estate
= Total taxable transfers
× Tax rates
= Tentative tax amount
− The unified credit
− Other credits
= Tax due

Taxable Gifts

Include

- Gifts of cash or FMV of noncash property
- Discount on sale of property to family member
- Reduction in interest on loans to family members at low rates

Exclude

- Donations to political organizations and charities
- Discounts given in negotiated transaction between independent parties
- Parental support of minor child
- Payments to college or health care provider for donee's tuition or medical care

Reduce by

- Marital deduction (unlimited)
- Gift exclusions

Taxable Gifts (continued)

Marital Deduction—Property given to a spouse is not taxable if spouse obtains either

- Complete ownership of property
- Right as trust beneficiary to income from property for remainder of beneficiary's life (Qualified Terminable Interest Property trust or QTIP trust)

Gift Exclusions

May exclude up to $14,000 per donee for 2017 if gift of present interest

Married couple making gift-splitting election may exclude twice as much per donee per year

Donee must generally receive present interest in gift

- Donee obtains an unrestricted right to the immediate use, possession, or enjoyment of property or the income from property

If donee is given a future interest, present value of gift is fully taxable (no $14,000 exclusion)

Taxable Estate

Gross estate—All property owned at time of death

Includes

- Proceeds from life insurance policies where deceased could change beneficiary
- Assets held in revocable trust
- Half of property owned jointly with spouse
- FMV of property × % of cost furnished by decedent if property held in joint tenancy with other than spouse
- Gifts of life insurance policies within three years of death
- Gift tax paid on all transfers made within three years of death

Valued at either

- Fair value at date of death
- Alternate valuation date (earlier of date of distribution from estate or six months after death)

Taxable Estate (continued)

Reduce by

- Charitable bequests
- Marital deduction
- Casualty losses
- Expenses and liabilities

Charitable bequests—Unlimited deduction for amounts left to charitable organizations

Marital deduction—Unlimited amount subject to same rules as gifts

Taxable Estate (continued)

Expenses and Liabilities—Deductions for

- Liabilities incurred prior to death
- Funeral costs
- Administrative fees
- Medical expenses
- State death taxes

Administrative fees may be deducted as either a liability on the estate tax return, or an expense deduction on the estate's income tax return.

Medical expenses incurred during decedent's lifetime may be deducted as claims against the estate, or as a medical deduction on the decedent's income tax return if paid within one year of death.

State death taxes are now only a deduction (no longer qualify as a credit).

Tax Due

Tentative Amount

Total taxable transfers
× Tax rates (from table)
= Tentative tax amount

Unified Credit

- Credit designed to remove relatively small gifts and estates from the transfer tax
- The exemption equivalent of the credit is $5.49 million, for both gift and estate tax purposes for 2017

Other Credits

Credit for death tax paid to foreign country on real estate owned in that country

Gift taxes paid on prior transfers (actually considered prepayment of liability rather than credit, but has same effect as credit to reduce balance due)

Generation-Skipping Tax

Owed on transfers (both gifts and inheritances) two or more generations below transferor

- Transfers to grandchildren, great-nieces, and great-nephews normally included
- Not applicable if immediate generation below is deceased (no GST on transfer to grandchild if the transferor's child is deceased)
- Exemption equivalent for GST same dollar amount as gift and estate tax exemption ($5.49 million for 2017)
- GST owed in addition to applicable gift and estate taxes

Property Received by Inheritance or Gift

Inheritance

Excluded from recipient's gross income

Basis—Fair market value reported on estate return

- Value at date of death (use this if no estate tax return filed)
- Value at alternate valuation date if elected on estate return (earlier of date of distribution to recipient or fair value exactly six months after death)

Holding period—automatically long-term

Gift

Receipt of gift excluded from recipient's gross income

Donee's basis for gain—Basis (and holding period) same as donor's

Donee's basis for loss—Lesser of gain basis, or FMV at date of gift

- If FMV at date of gift is used to determine a loss, then holding period begins on date of gift
- If donee's selling price is below gain basis and above loss basis, then no gain or loss

Taxation of Estates and Trusts

Estates

Results from death of individual

- Assets become part of estate
- Investments generate income
- Estate taxed on earnings

Trusts

Types of Trusts

Simple trusts

- Must distribute all income each year
- Cannot make charitable contributions
- Cannot distribute trust corpus (principal)

Complex trusts—all others

Trust Operations

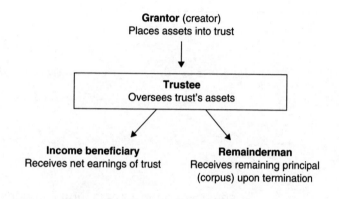

Grantor (creator)
Places assets into trust

↓

Trustee
Oversees trust's assets

Income beneficiary
Receives net earnings of trust

Remainderman
Receives remaining principal
(corpus) upon termination

Taxation of Trusts

Grantor (revocable) trust

- Creator has right to withdraw assets at any time
- Earnings taxed to creator (as if trust did not exist)

Irrevocable trust

- Creator generally may not withdraw assets
- Trust taxed separately from creator or beneficiaries

Computing Taxable Income of Trusts and Estates

Gross income
- – Deductions
- – Exemption
- = Taxable income

Gross Income

Same rules as for individuals

Includes

- Rents
- Dividends
- Interest
- Capital gains

Deductions

Generally similar to those available to individual

In addition

- Charitable contributions—No limit on amount
- Management fees—Fees paid to trustee or executor
  - Trust or estate may have nontaxable income
  - Proportionate amount of fees not deductible
- Distributions paid—Amounts paid to beneficiaries

Exemption

Estate—$600

Simple trust—$300

Complex trust—$100

Distributable Net Income (DNI)

DNI is maximum amount of distribution that can be taxed to income beneficiary

- Includes most income and expense items on trust tax return
- Includes municipal bond interest
- Does not include net capital gains (allocated to principal)

Taxation of Beneficiaries

Not taxed on inheritance of estate property

Taxed on distributions of income up to DNI

CORPORATE TAXATION

Corporate Income Tax

Section 351 Transfer to Controlled Corporation

No gain or loss is recognized if property is transferred to a corporation solely in exchange for stock if the transferors of property (in the aggregate) control the corporation

- *Property* includes cash and everything but services
- *Control* is the ownership of at least 80% of the corporation's stock

Services for Stock

Taxable transaction

- Taxable compensation to shareholder = FMV of stock
- Shareholder basis for stock = FMV
- Corporation has expense or asset = FMV of stock

Property for Stock

Generally a nontaxable transaction

- Whenever shareholders providing cash and property have total ownership ≥ 80%
- Shareholder basis for stock = Basis for asset given (exchanged basis) + Gain recognized − boot received
- Corporation basis for asset = Same as shareholder's basis + Gain recognized to shareholder

Taxable transaction

- When shareholders providing cash and property have ownership < 80%
- Shareholder recognizes gain or loss = FMV − Basis
- Shareholder basis for stock = FMV
- Corporation basis for asset = FMV

Computing Corporate Income Tax

Gross income

−	Deductions
=	Taxable income
×	Tax rate
=	Preliminary tax liability
+	Personal holding company tax
+	Accumulated earnings tax
+	Alternative minimum tax
=	Total tax liability
−	Credits
=	Net tax liability
−	Estimated payments
=	Tax due (or refund)

Gross Income

General concept of gross income applies to a corporation

- Corporation never recognizes gain or loss when it issues its own stock
- Corporation's net capital gain is taxed at ordinary rates
- No income is recognized by a corporation on receipt of capital contribution
- If received from a shareholder, property has a transferred basis
- If received from a non shareholder, property has a zero basis

Deductions

Deductible expenses include

- Ordinary and reasonable operating expenses
- Compensation costs including wages and bonuses
- Employer payroll taxes
- Fringe benefits including health and life insurance when employee selects beneficiary
- Interest on business indebtedness
- Bad debts when a specific debt is written off
- Meals and entertainment × 50%
- Straight-line amortization of goodwill over 15 years
- May deduct up to $5,000 of organizational expenditures (reduced by excess of costs over $50,000) and amortize remaining costs over 180 months beginning with the month that business begins. *Business investigation and start-up costs (advertising, employee training) are subject to same rule.*

Deductions (continued)

Nondeductible expenses include

- Fines, penalties, and punitive damages
- Compensation in excess of $1,000,000 paid to each of five highest paid executives
- Accrued compensation and charitable pledges not paid within 2½ months after year-end
- Interest expense on debt used to acquire nontaxable investments
- Premiums on key person insurance if company is beneficiary
- Club dues
- Cost of issuing, printing, and selling stock

Charitable Contributions

1) Generally deductible when paid, but accrual method corporation can elect to deduct when accrued if authorized by board of directors before year-end and paid within 2½ months after year-end

2) Excess carried forward five years

3) Deduction *limited* to 10% of contribution base which is TI before charitable contributions, DRD, NOL carryback, capital loss carryback, and domestic production activities deduction

Dividends-Received Deduction

1) Determine % for deduction
   - Corporation's ownership < 20%—Deduct 70%
   - Ownership ≥ 20% but < 80%—Deduct 80%
   - Ownership ≥ 80%—Deduct 100% if consolidated tax return not filed
2) Apply % to dividends or taxable income before deduction, whichever is lower
3) Exception—If % × dividends > taxable income, use entire amount, resulting in loss

Does not apply to

- Dividends from a foreign corporation
- Dividends from a tax-exempt organization

Supplemental Tax Schedules

Corporations complete two supplemental schedules on their tax returns

- **Schedule M-1** reconciles book income to taxable income
- **Schedule M-2** reconciles beginning to ending retained earnings per books
- **Schedule M-3** is a more detailed version of the M-1 required for corporations with total assets in excess of $10 million

Alternative Minimum Tax (AMT)

Regular taxable income

±   Preferences and adjustments

=   Pre-ACE alternative minimum taxable income (AMTI)

±   ACE adjustment [75% of difference between pre-ACE AMTI and adjusted current earnings (ACE)]

=   Alternative minimum taxable income

−   Exemption ($40,000 less 25% of AMTI over $150,000)

=   Base

×   Tax rate (20%)

=   Tentative tax before credits

−   Foreign tax credit

=   Tentative tax

−   Regular tax liability

=   AMT

Alternative Minimum Tax (continued)

Adjustments and preferences are added back to or deducted from taxable income in computing AMTI. They include

- Interest on private activity bonds
- Difference between regular tax 200% DB depreciation and 150% DB depreciation allowed for AMT purposes (Property for which a taxpayer elects out of bonus depreciation is not subject to an AMT depreciation adjustment, effective for property placed in service after 2015)
- Installment method can't be used for sale of inventory-type items
- Adjusted current earnings (ACE) adjustment

ACE = Adjusted current earnings

Pre-ACE AMTI

\+ Nontaxable revenues

− Nondeductible expenses

= ACE

Alternative Minimum Tax (continued)

Adjustments to pre-ACE AMTI to compute ACE include adding

- **S**eventy percent dividends received deduction
- **L**ife Insurance proceeds
- **M**unicipal bond interest on general obligation bonds

*There's a **slim** chance that you'll avoid the AMT*

ACE adjustment = 75% × (ACE – pre-ACE AMTI)

AMTI is reduced by the **exemption** amount

Exemption = $40,000 – 25% × (AMTI – $150,000)

Resulting base amount × AMT tax rate = Tentative minimum tax

Tentative minimum tax – Regular income tax = AMT

- If tentative minimum tax > regular income tax, it increases the amount of tax paid
- AMT paid in current year is carried forward as credit to reduce regular taxes in future years

Personal Holding Company (PHC) Tax

Corporation is subject to PHC tax if two conditions apply

1) Interest, dividends, rents, royalties, or personal service contracts > 60% of gross income
2) Five or fewer shareholders own > 50% stock

PHC tax

- Self-assessed on Schedule PH which is attached to Form 1120
- PHC tax = Undistributed PHC income × 20%
- Added to regular tax
- Can be reduced by actual and consent dividends

Consent dividends—Hypothetical dividends that are treated as paid on last day of corporation's tax year. Shareholders report dividend income and increase stock basis by the amount of consent dividend.

Accumulated Earnings Tax

The accumulated earnings tax is not self assessed

- Does not apply to PHCs
- Generally assessed on earnings accumulated in excess of reasonable business needs
- Corporation allowed to deduct accumulated earnings credit which is greater of
  - Earnings needed to satisfy reasonable business needs, or
  - Minimum credit of $250,000 (or $150,000 for service corporation) less AEP at beginning of year
- Accumulated earnings tax = Accumulated taxable income × 20%
- Added to regular tax
- Can be reduced by actual and consent dividends

Affiliated Corporation Transactions

Affiliated parent-subsidiary relationship exists when one corporation owns at least 80% of total voting power and total value of another corporation's outstanding stock

- Companies may elect to file consolidated return
- Intercompany dividends and gains and losses on intercompany transactions are eliminated in consolidation process

Non-liquidating Distributions to Shareholders

Property Distributions

Treated as dividends when paid from earnings and profits (E&P)

- Can be paid out of current E&P computed at end of tax year, even if accumulated E&P is negative amount
- Can be paid out of accumulated E&P, even if current E&P is negative amount to extent of accumulated E&P still remaining at distribution date

Distribution in excess of E&P

- Nontaxable return of stock basis
- Capital gain to extent in excess of stock basis

Property Distributions

When noncash property is distributed

- Corporation recognizes gain if FMV > basis
- Corporation not permitted to recognize loss if FMV < basis
- Shareholder recognizes dividend equal to FMV of property – liabilities assumed
- Shareholder's basis for property received = FMV

Corporate Complete Liquidation

Distributions of assets upon termination are liquidating distributions

- Corporation recognizes gain or loss when FMV ≠ basis in assets distributed
- Shareholder generally recognizes capital gain or loss when FMV ≠ basis in stock

Upon liquidation of an at least 80%-owned subsidiary

- Subsidiary recognizes no gain or loss on distribution of assets to parent
- Parent recognizes no gain or loss on cancellation of stock
- Parent's basis for assets = same as subsidiary's basis (transferred basis)
- Tax attributes of subsidiary (E&P, net operating losses, credits) carry over to parent

Corporate Reorganizations

Mergers and Acquisitions

Assets, liabilities, and tax attributes of acquired corporation are transferred to acquiring corporation.

When shareholders receive stock in acquiring corporation for shares in acquired corporation

- No gain or loss recognized except to extent of cash or other boot received
- Basis for new shares = Basis for old shares + Gain recognized – Boot received

Spin-offs and split-offs

One corporation divides into two or more separate corporations

Section 1244 Stock

Treatment as section 1244 stock applies if two conditions are met

1. Stock was issued as part of first $1,000,000 of capital raised by corporation
2. Shareholder must be the original holder of stock, and an individual or partnership

Sale or exchange of section 1244 stock

- Gains treated as capital gains
- Losses treated as ordinary deduction to maximum of $50,000 per year ($100,000 on joint return). Loss in excess of limitation treated as capital loss.

S Corporations

S Corporation—A Pass-Through Entity

Eligibility Requirements

S corporation status requires all of the following:

- Number of shareholders ≤ 100
- Husband and wife are treated as a single shareholder (all descendants and spouses within six generations of a single ancestor may elect to be treated as a single shareholder)
- Shareholders limited to individuals, estates, and trusts with one income beneficiary
- Only one class of stock (voting and nonvoting stock are treated as a single class of stock)

Election

Corporation must elect S corporation status.

- All shareholders must elect unanimously
- All eligibility requirements must be met on date of election
- Election made during first 2½ months of tax year is generally effective for that year
- Election made after first 2½ months of tax year is generally effective for following year

Taxation of S Corporations

S corporation is a pass-through entity.

S corporation must file Form 1120S tax return and must file Form K-1 for each shareholder indicating each shareholder's share of income and expenses.

S corporation's income and expenses **pass through** to individual shareholders.

- All ordinary income and deduction items can be netted with the net amount passed through to shareholders
- All items having special tax characteristics must be separately stated when passed through to shareholders
- Each item is combined with comparable items recognized by the shareholder

S Corporation Earnings

Pass-Through Item	Tax Treatment
Capital gains and losses	Combined with shareholder's capital gains and losses
Section 1231 gains and losses	Combined with shareholder's Sec. 1231 gains and losses
Charitable contributions	Subject to 30% and 50% limitations at shareholders level
Interest and dividend income and related expenses	Investment interest expense deductible to extent of net investment income
Net rent and royalty income	Subject to passive activity loss limitations

S Corporation Earnings (continued)

Pass-Through Item	Tax Treatment
Section 179 deduction	Subject to dollar limitation at both corporate and shareholder level
Tax credits	Limited to shareholder's tax liability
Tax-exempt income and related expenses	Income exempt to shareholders Expenses not deductible by shareholder
Tax preferences and adjustments	Used to compute shareholder's AMT
Net all ordinary and deduction items (non separately stated income or loss)	Treated as ordinary income or loss Loss deduction limited to shareholder's stock and debt basis

Shareholder's Basis

A shareholder's basis for S corporation stock is adjusted in the following order

Initial basis

+   Share of income (including exempt income)

−   Distributions received

−   Share of loss (including nondeductible expenses)

=   Basis for stock

- All S corporation income and deduction items are allocated per-share, per-day
- A shareholder who disposes of stock is treated as the shareholder for the day of disposition
- Basis adjustments for distributions are taken into account before expenses and losses
- Distributions to shareholders are generally a nontaxable return of stock basis because they represent income that has already been taxed to the shareholder

Conversion from C to S Corporation

An S corporation is generally not taxed on its income

When a C corporation elects S corporation status, it may be subject to

1) Built-in gains (BIG) tax—Applies when company sells appreciated built-in gain assets within 5 years of election
- S corporation pays tax at highest corporate rate (35%) on net recognized built-in gain

FMV of assets at effective date of election

  − Adjusted basis of assets

  = Net unrealized built-in gain

2) Tax on excess net passive investment income—Applies when investment income > 25% of gross receipts from all sources and corporation has AE&P from C years
- S corporation pays tax at highest corporate rate (35%) on lesser of passive investment income in excess of 25%, or taxable income
- Gains on sales of stocks or securities not considered passive investment income

Termination of S Corporation Status

Either of the following will cause a corporation to lose its S corporation status:

- Shareholders owning > 50% of shares vote to revoke election
- Fail eligibility requirements. Termination is effective on date eligibility requirement failed.

Once terminated, corporation must generally wait five years to elect again

Foreign Tax Credit

Reduces US income tax for amount of income taxes paid to foreign jurisdictions

Credit = smaller of

- Amount of foreign tax paid
- Foreign taxable income ÷ Total taxable income × Total US tax liability

PARTNERSHIP TAXATION

Formation of Partnerships

Contribution of Assets

When a partner contributes cash or property for a partnership interest, the transfer is generally nontaxable

- Partner's basis in partnership = basis for assets contributed
- Partnership's basis for assets = partner's basis (transferred basis)

Contribution of Services

When a partner contributes services for an interest in partnership capital, the FMV of the partnership interest received is taxable as compensation

- Partner's recognized income and basis for partnership interest = FMV
- Partnership recognizes expense or asset = FMV

Changes in Liabilities

Changes in liabilities are treated as a change in the flow of money and either increase or decrease a partner's basis

- Increased by an increase in partnership liabilities, or an increase in individual liabilities (treat as a contribution of money and increase basis)
- Decreased by a decrease in partnership liabilities, or a decrease in individual liabilities (treat as a distribution of money and decrease basis)

Partnership's Tax Year

Adoption or change of partnership tax year restricted by tax years used by its partners

1) Adopt same tax year as used by partners owning > 50% of partnership interests
2) If partners owning > 50% of interests do not have same year, adopt tax year used by partners owning ≥ 5% interest if all have same tax year
3) If all partners with ≥ 5% interest do not have same tax year, use year that results in least deferral of income to partners

Partner's Basis

Initial basis

±   Changes in liabilities

+   Partner's share of income (including tax-exempt income)

−   Distributions (cash + the adjusted basis of property)

−   Partner's share of expenses and losses (including nondeductible items)

=   Partner's basis for partnership interest

Initial basis = cash, adjusted basis of property, and FMV of services contributed

Partner's share of income or loss = partner's proportionate share of all of partnership's income and expenses, regardless of nature

Distributions = cash and adjusted basis of property distributed to partner

Partner's proportionate share of partnership's liabilities are added to basis

Partner's liabilities that are transferred to the partnership reduce basis

Taxation of Partnerships

Partnerships are pass-through entities, not taxable entities

Reporting is similar to S corporations

- Partnership files Form 1065 tax return
- Starting for the 2016 tax year, Form 1065 is due by 15th day of the third month following end of tax year
- Prepare form K-1 for each partner indicating partner's share of income and expenses
- Partnership's income and expenses pass through to partners
- Separate items into ordinary income and deductions items which can be netted, and items having special tax characteristics which must be separately passed through to partners to retain those characteristics
- Partner combines with similar items incurred individually from other sources
- Combined amounts subject to normal limitations at partner level

Guaranteed Payments to Partners

Guaranteed payments to partners are amounts partners are entitled to regardless of partnership's profit or loss

May be

- Compensation for services performed
- Payment based on capital investment in partnership

Taxed as follows

- Partner recognizes ordinary income (generally self-employment income)
- Partnership deducts in calculating partnership ordinary income or loss

Partners' Distributive Shares

Partners report their distributive share of all partnership items for the partnership year that ends with (or within) their taxable year

Items are deemed to pass through on the last day of partnership tax year

Distributions

Non-liquidating Distributions

Cash distributed

- Reduces partner's basis for partnership interest
- Taxable to extent cash distribution > basis

Noncash property distributed

- Basis to partner = lower of partnership's basis for property or partner's basis for partnership interest
- Basis for partnership interest reduced by partner's basis for distributed property
- No gain or loss recognized by partnership or partners

Liquidating Distributions

Distributions to partner that terminate partner's entire partnership interest

Cash distributions

- Difference between amount received and partner's basis for partnership interest = recognized gain or loss
- Remaining basis in partnership = $0

Noncash property distributions

- Basis of property to partner = former basis for partnership interest
- Remaining basis in partnership = $0
- Generally no gain or loss recognized

Sale of Partnership Interest

Determining Gain or Loss

Amount realized from sale

- Basis for partnership interest

= Realized gain or loss

  - Amount realized = Cash + FMV of property received + Assumption of selling partner's share of partnership liabilities by buyer
  - Include partner's share of liabilities in computing the partner's basis for partnership interest

Taxation of Gains and Losses

Gain or loss divided into 2 segments

  - Ordinary income will result to extent of partner's share of unrealized receivables and appreciated inventory (unrealized receivables include recapture potential in depreciable assets)
  - Any remaining amount is capital gain or loss

Termination

Partnership terminates and its tax year closes when either

- Partnership no longer has at least two partners, or stops doing business
- More than 50% of total partnership interests are sold within a 12-month period

INDEX